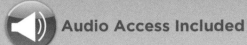

Hal•Leonard
EASY INSTRUMENTAL PLAY-ALONG

🔊 Audio Access Included

CHRISTMAS CAROLS
FOR KEYBOARD PERCUSSION

CONTENTS

To access audio visit:
www.halleonard.com/mylibrary

Enter Code
7498-9572-5162-2372

Audio Arrangements by Peter Deneff
Tracking, mixing, and mastering by BeatHouse Music

ISBN 978-1-4803-9610-4

HAL•LEONARD®
CORPORATION

7777 W. BLUEMOUND RD. P.O. BOX 13819 MILWAUKEE, WI 53213

In Australia Contact:
Hal Leonard Australia Pty. Ltd.
4 Lentara Court
Cheltenham, Victoria, 3192 Australia
Email: ausadmin@halleonard.com.au

Visit Hal Leonard Online at
www.halleonard.com

ANGELS WE HAVE HEARD ON HIGH

Traditional French Carol

CHRIST WAS BORN ON CHRISTMAS DAY

Traditional

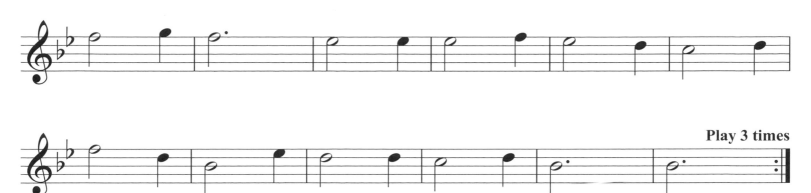

Play 3 times

COME, ALL YE SHEPHERDS

Traditional Czech Text
Traditional Moravian Melody

COME, THOU LONG-EXPECTED JESUS

Words by CHARLES WESLEY
Music by ROWLAND HUGH PRICHARD

GOOD CHRISTIAN MEN, REJOICE

14th Century Latin Text
14th Century German Melody

JINGLE BELLS

Words and Music by
J. PIERPONT

ON CHRISTMAS NIGHT

Sussex Carol

rit.

UP ON THE HOUSETOP

Words and Music by
B.R. HANBY

8

JOLLY OLD ST. NICHOLAS

Traditional 19th Century American Carol

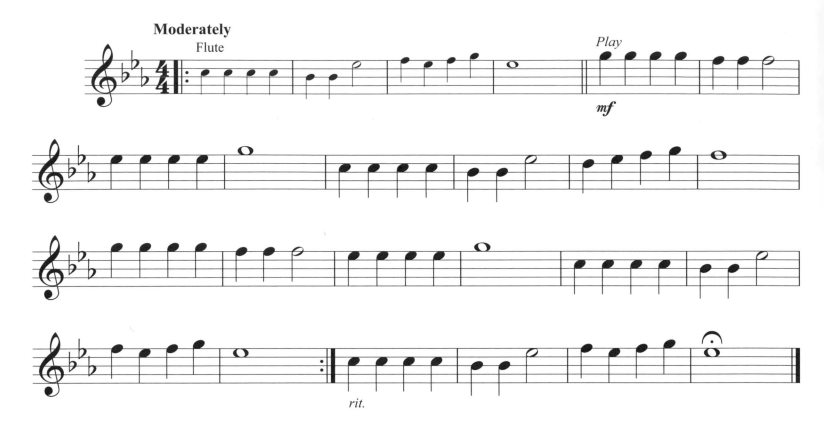

LO, HOW A ROSE E'ER BLOOMING

15th Century German Carol

WE'LL RANT AND WE'LL ROAR 3

52

WE'LL RANT AND WE'LL ROAR 2

WE'LL RANT AND WE'LL ROAR

Newfoundland Folk Song
Arr. Timothy Campbell (ASCAP)

MOLLY MALONE 3

MOLLY MALONE 2

MOLLY MALONE

Newfoundland Folk Song
Arr. Timothy Campbell (ASCAP)

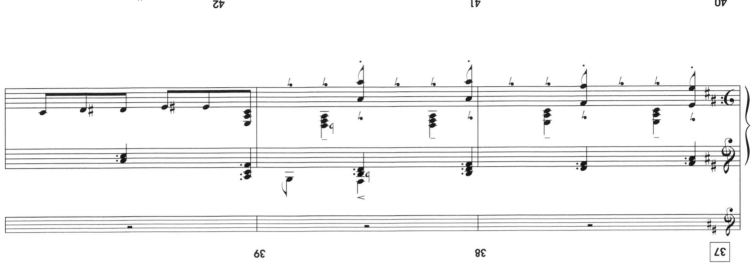

THE IRISH WASHERWOMAN 3

THE IRISH WASHERWOMAN 2

THE IRISH WASHERWOMAN

Irish Folk Song
Arr. Timothy Campbell (ASCAP)

Pedal harmonically throughout

MOUNTAINS OF MOURNE 3

MOUNTAINS OF MOURNE 2

42

MOUNTAINS OF MOURNE

Irish Folk Song
Arr. Timothy Campbell (ASCAP)

MRS. MURPHY'S CHOWDER 2

MRS. MURPHY'S CHOWDER

Irish Folk Song
Arr. Timothy Campbell (ASCAP)

WHEN IRISH EYES ARE SMILING 3

WHEN IRISH EYES ARE SMILING 2

WHEN IRISH EYES ARE SMILING

Irish Folk Song
Arr. Timothy Campbell (ASCAP)

Pedal harmonically throughout

LUKEY'S BOAT 3

CMP 1044-05 Violin

LUKEY'S BOAT 2

LUKEY'S BOAT

Newfoundland Folk Song
Arr. Timothy Campbell (ASCAP)

TOO-RA-LOO-RA-LOO-RAL 2

TOO-RA-LOO-RA-LOO-RAL

(That's An Irish Lullaby)

Irish Folk Song
Arr. Timothy Campbell (ASCAP)

LOCH LOMOND 3

LOCH LOMOND 2

LOCH LOMOND

Scottish Folk Song
Arr. Timothy Campbell (ASCAP)

Pedal harmonically throughout

1ST RECITAL SERIES

HIGHLIGHTS INCLUDE

Carefully graded solos from Very Easy up to Early Intermediate levels

Professionally recorded Demonstration/Accompaniment CD included

Practice and perform accompanied by the CD or with a live piano player

Demo tracks help the player develop proper performance practice

Original compositions by many of today's finest composers

12 outstanding solos in a wide variety of musical styles

Arrangements of great classic melodies

Excellent literature for concert, contest, church, or home enjoyment

Perfect for private lesson studios

Piano accompaniment book available

Including works of:
- James Curnow
- Craig Alan
- Douglas Court
- Mike Hannickel
- Timothy Johnson
- Ann Lindsay

Position 1- 3

Available books:

Violin	CMP 0841-03-400
Viola	CMP 0842-03-400
Cello	CMP 0843-03-400

Piano accompaniments:

Piano/Violin	CMP 0844-03-400
Piano/Viola	CMP 0845-03-400
Piano/Cello	CMP 0846-03-400

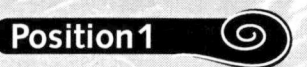

Selected by James Curnow

Position 1

EASY GREAT CAROLS

Easy Great Carols contains carols from around the world, including both sacred and whimsical selections. They are delightfully arranged in fresh settings by some of the foremost arrangers in the instrumental field. Written with the intermediate instrumental soloist in mind, this product is designed to be accessible, yet interesting. The accompaniment CD (included in the solo book) provides a demonstration performance of each solo. It also allows the soloist to practice or perform with the CD when an accompanist is not available.

CMP 0975-05-400

WE'LL RANT AND WE'LL ROAR

Newfoundland Folk Song
Arr. Timothy Campbell (ASCAP)

30 31

MOLLY MALONE

Newfoundland Folk Song
Arr. **Timothy Campbell** (ASCAP)

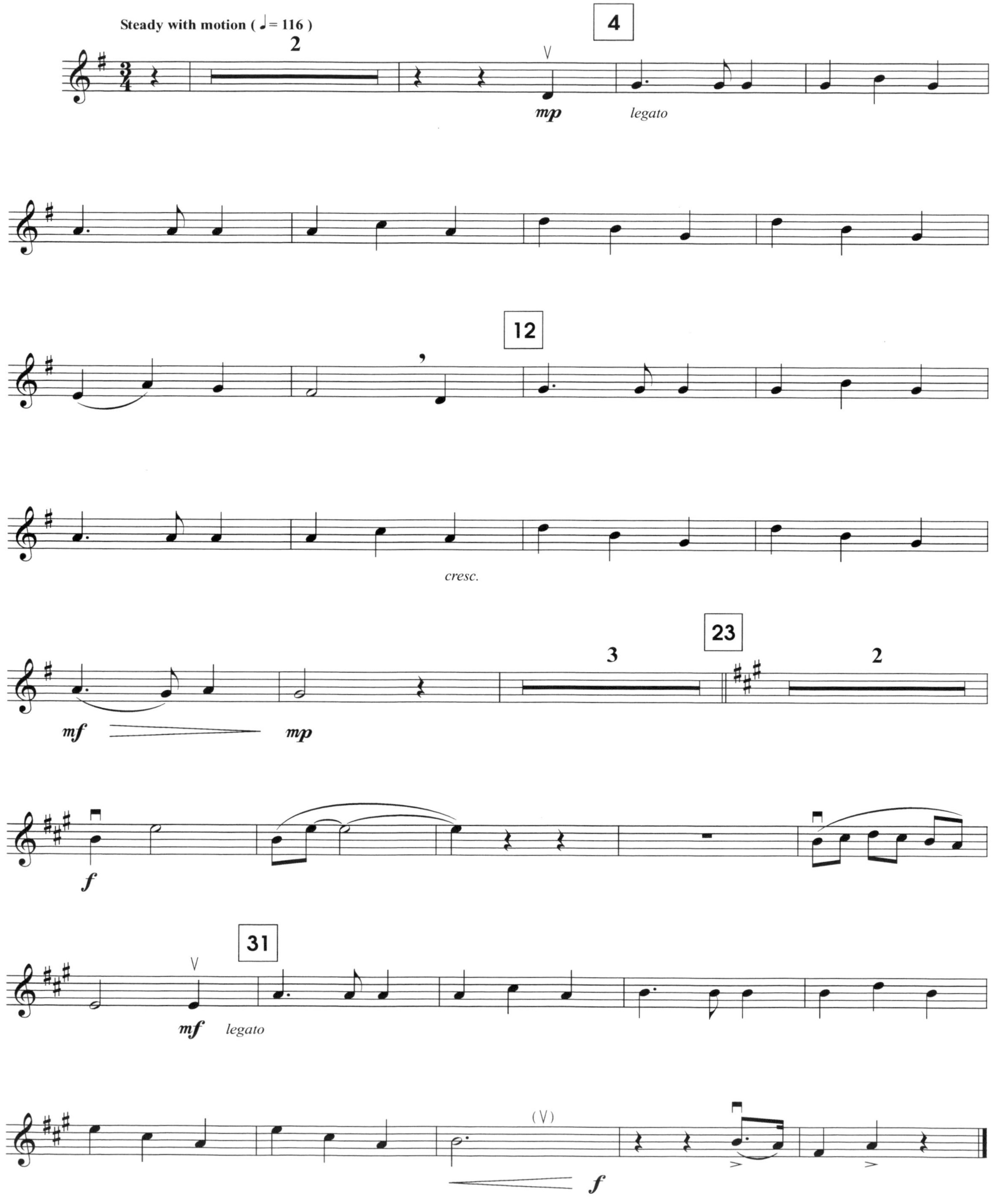

THE IRISH WASHERWOMAN

Irish Folk Song
Arr. Timothy Campbell (ASCAP)

With spirit (♩. = 72)

MOUNTAINS OF MOURNE

26 27

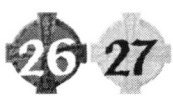

Irish Folk Song
Arr. Timothy Campbell (ASCAP)

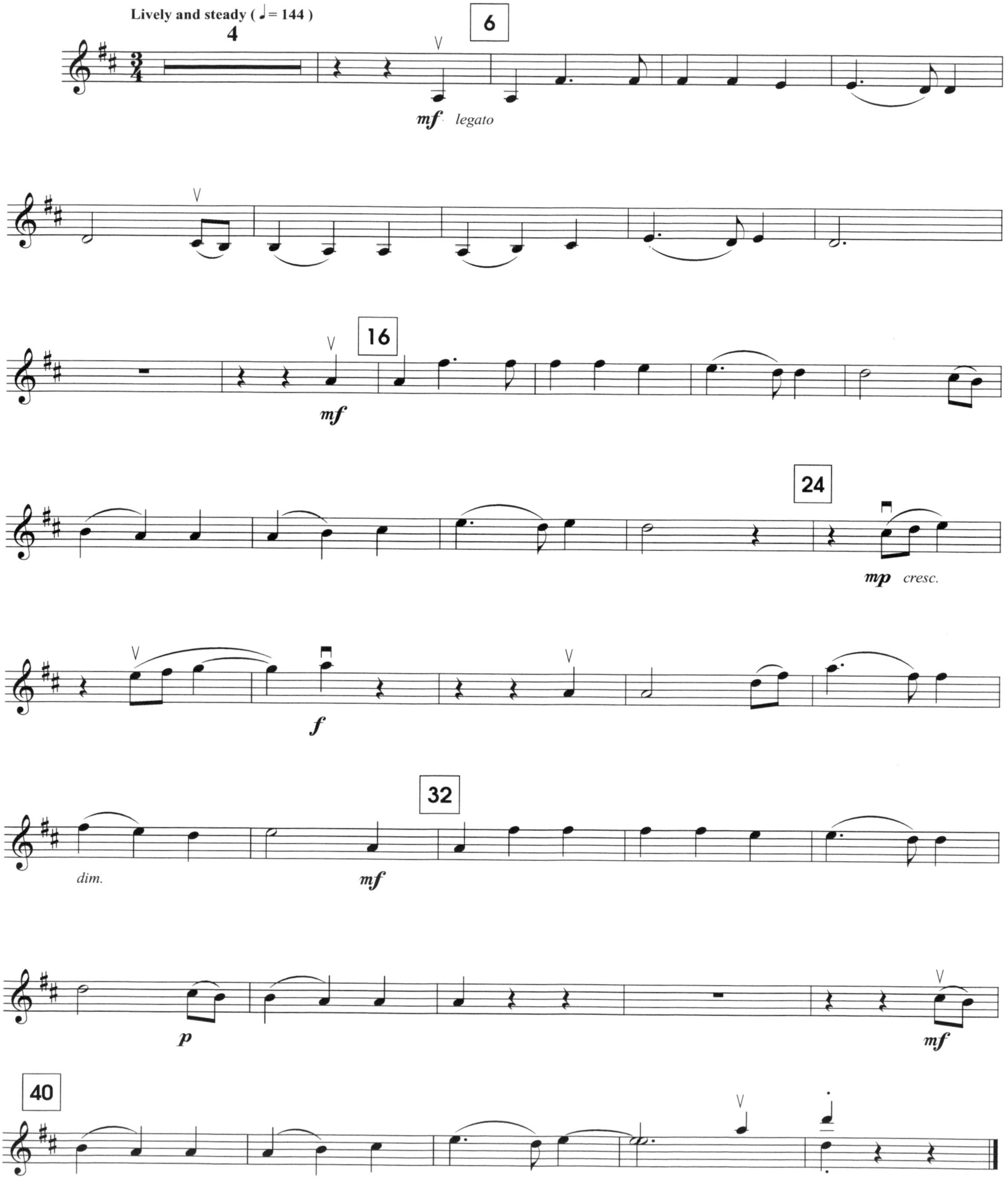

MRS. MURPHY'S CHOWDER

Irish Folk Song
Arr. Timothy Campbell (ASCAP)

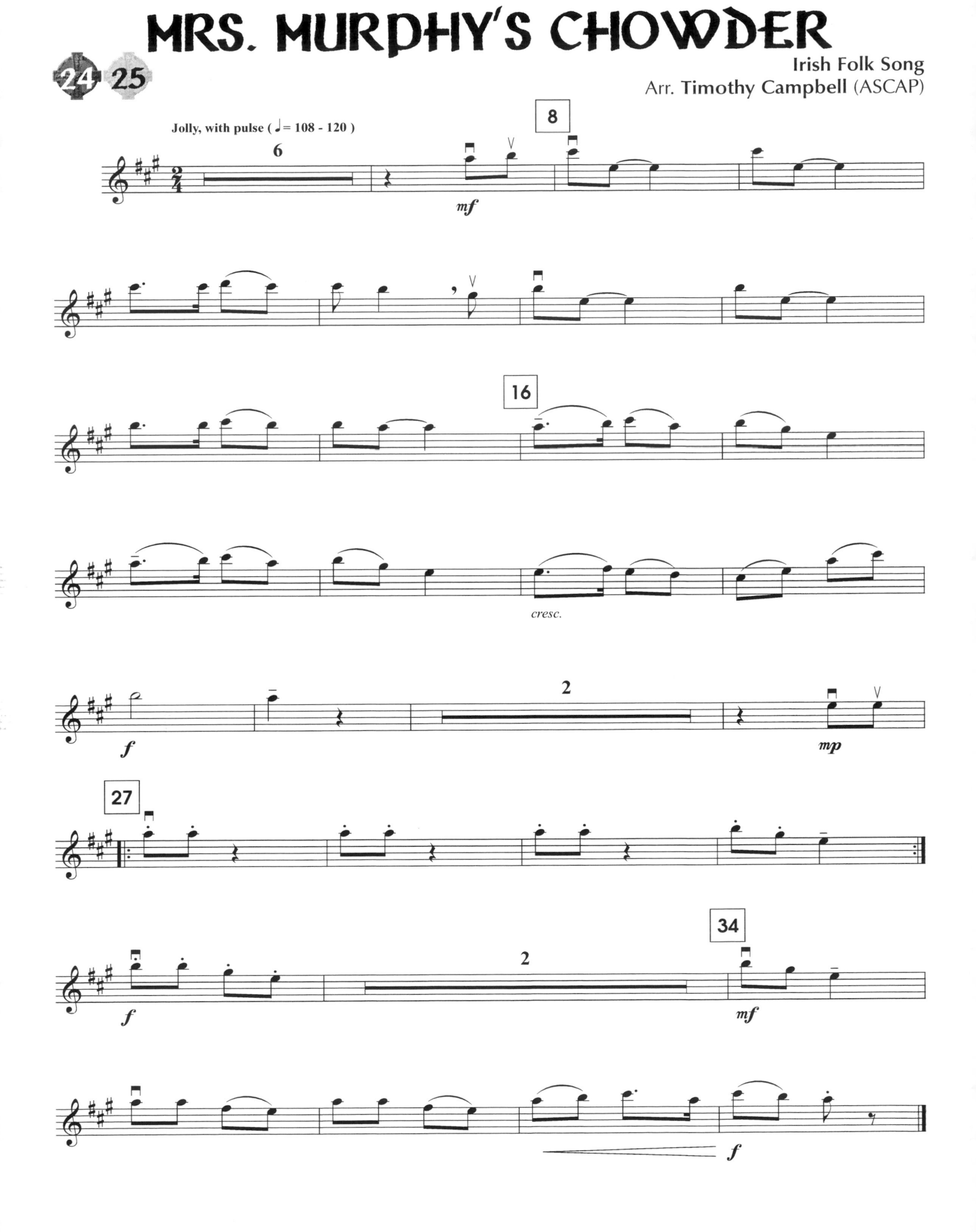

WHEN IRISH EYES ARE SMILING

Irish Folk Song
Arr. Timothy Campbell (ASCAP)

LUKEY'S BOAT

Newfoundland Folk Song
Arr. Timothy Campbell (ASCAP)

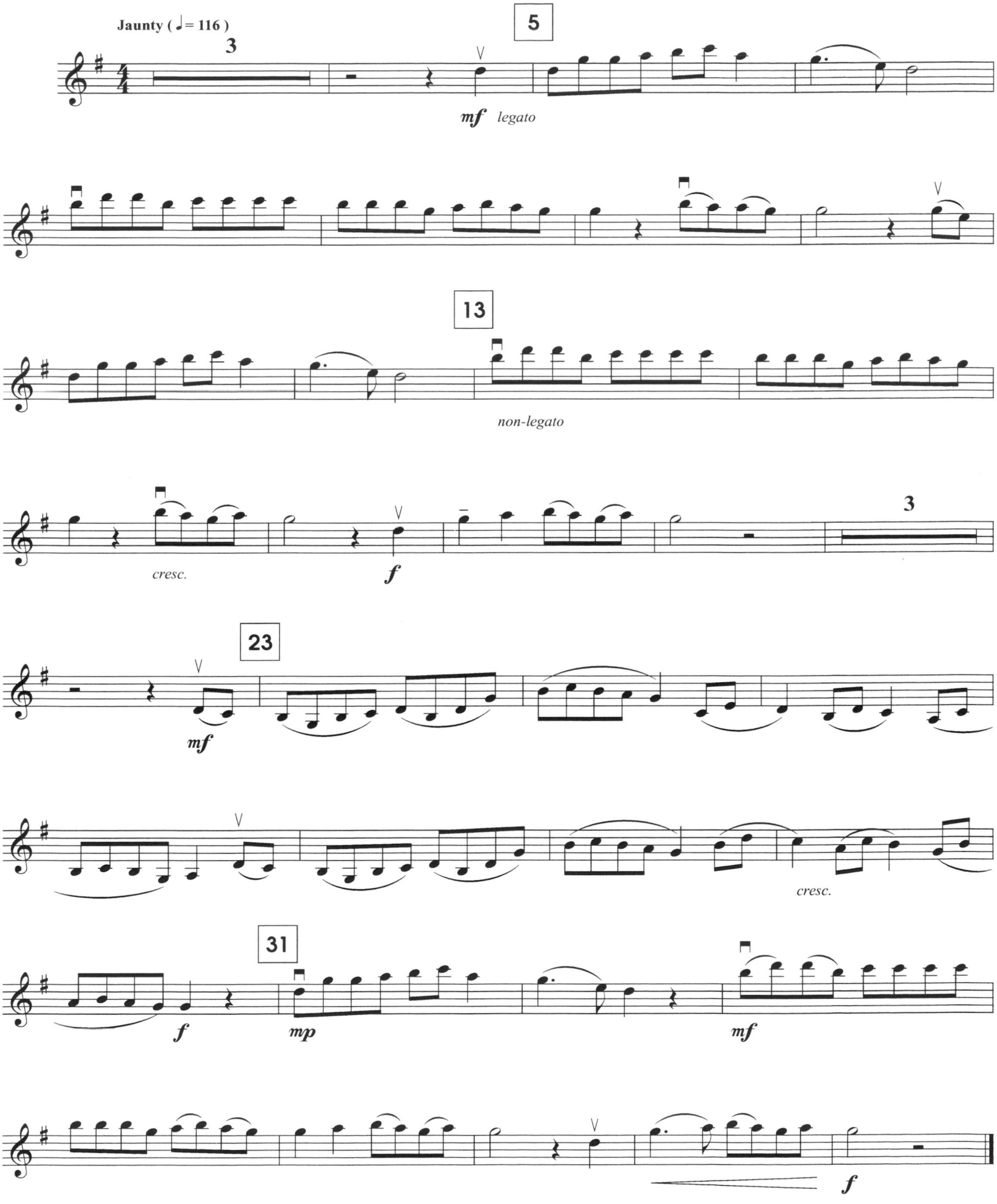

TOO-RA-LOO-RA-LOO-RAL

(That's An Irish Lullaby)

Irish Folk Song
Arr. Timothy Campbell (ASCAP)

At a walking tempo (♩ = 80)

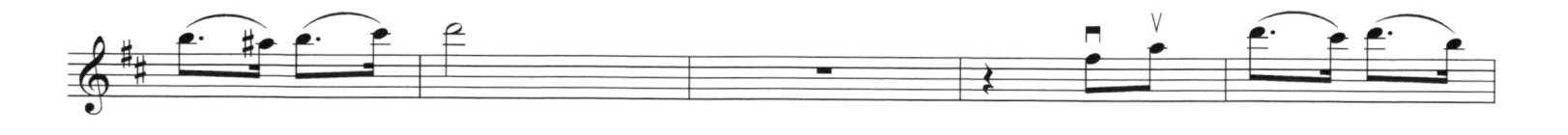

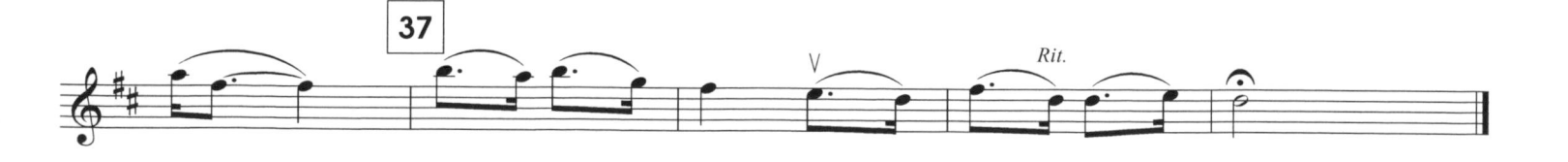

16 17

LOCH LOMOND

Scottish Folk Song
Arr. Timothy Campbell (ASCAP)

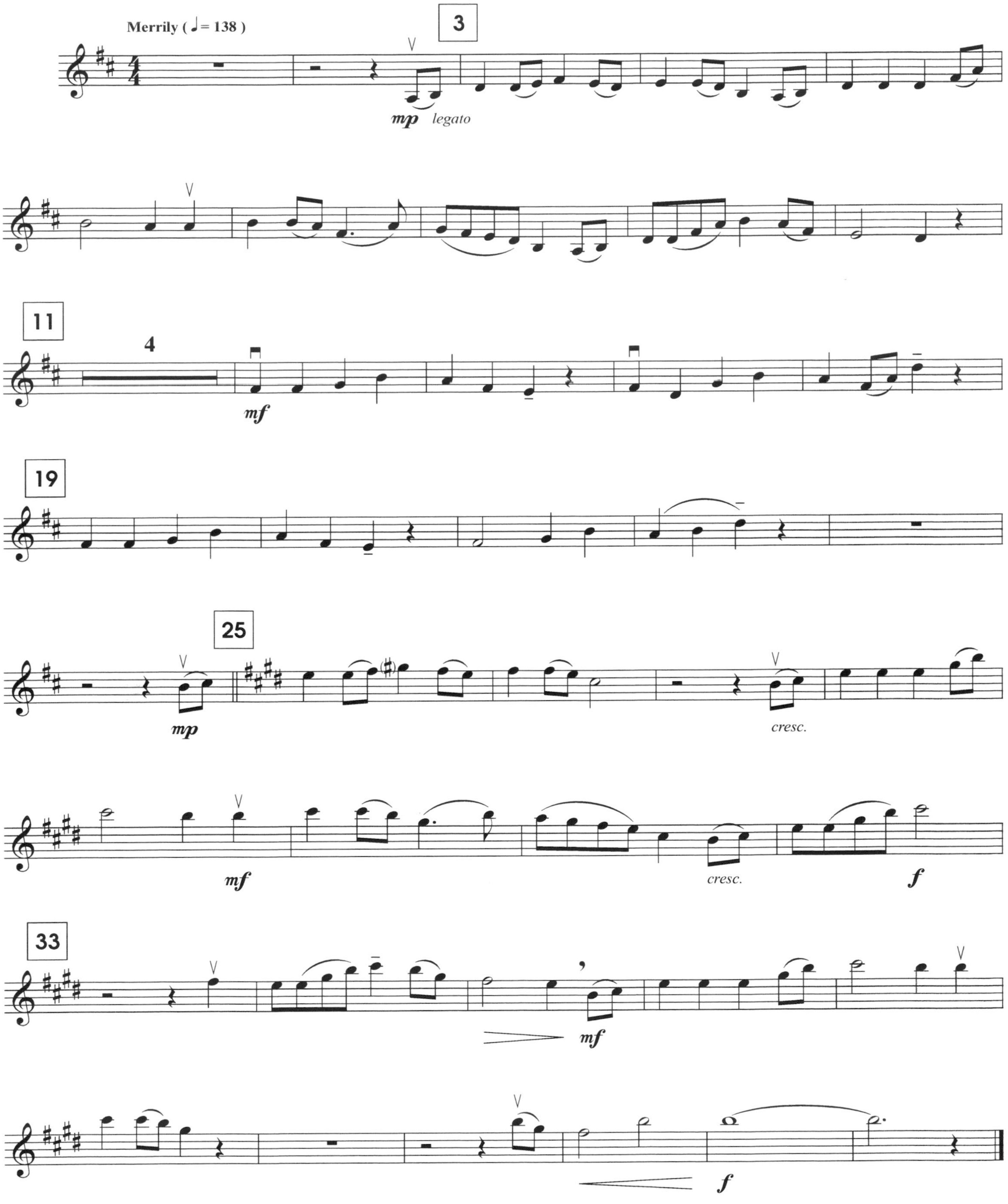

I'S THE B'Y

Newfoundland Folk Song
Arr. **Timothy Campbell** (ASCAP)

Copyright © 2005 by **Curnow Music Press, Inc.**

I'LL TELL ME MA

Irish Folk Song
Arr. Timothy Campbell (ASCAP)

THE ASH GROVE

Welsh Folk Song
Arr. Timothy Campbell (ASCAP)

Copyright © 2005 by Curnow Music Press, Inc.

Copyright © 2005 by **Curnow Music Press, Inc.**

BELIEVE ME, IF ALL THOSE ENDEARING YOUNG CHARMS

Irish Folk Song
Arr. Timothy Campbell (ASCAP)

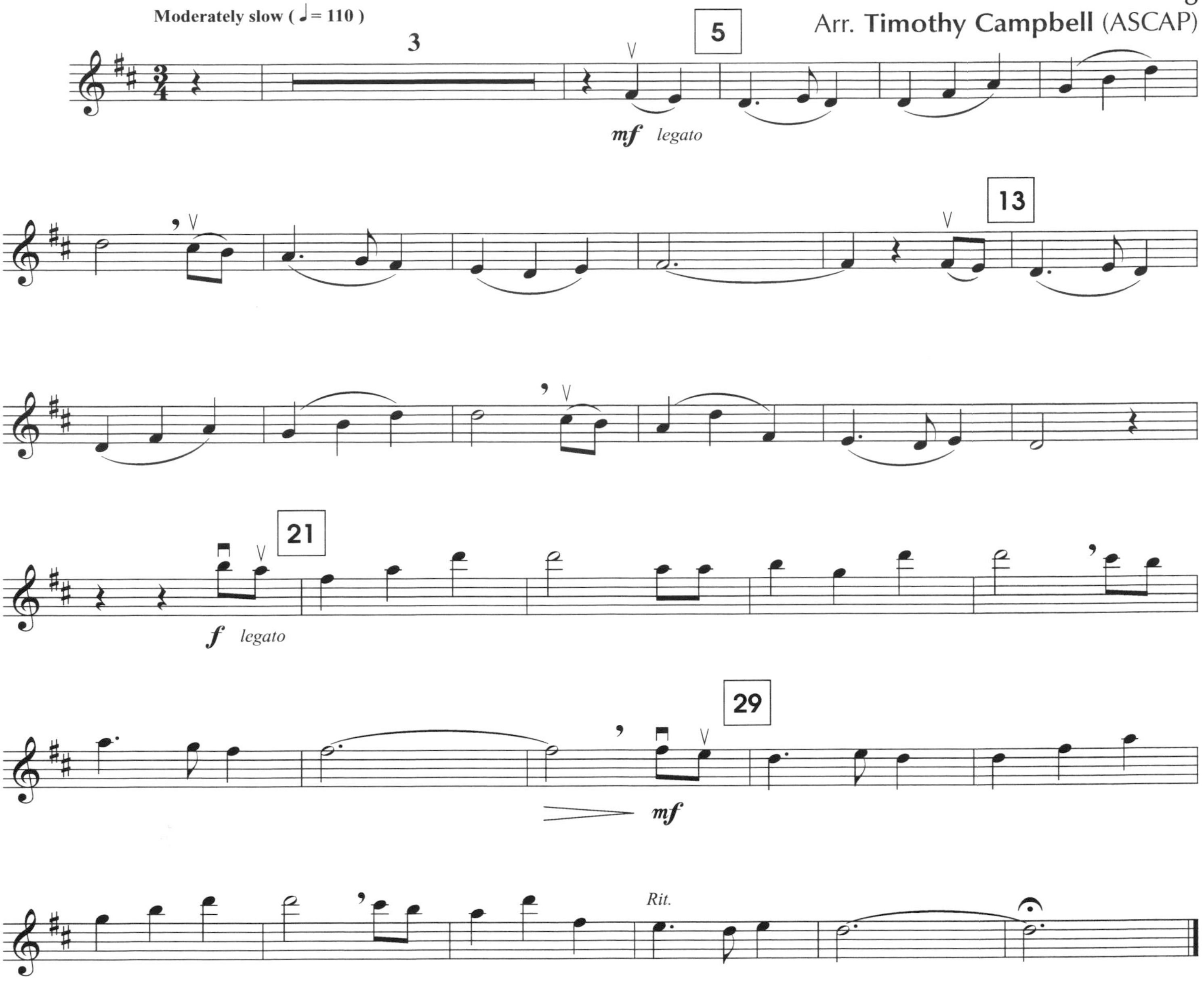

Moderately slow (♩ = 110)

JACK WAS EVERY INCH A SAILOR

Newfoundland Folk Song
Arr. James Curnow (ASCAP)

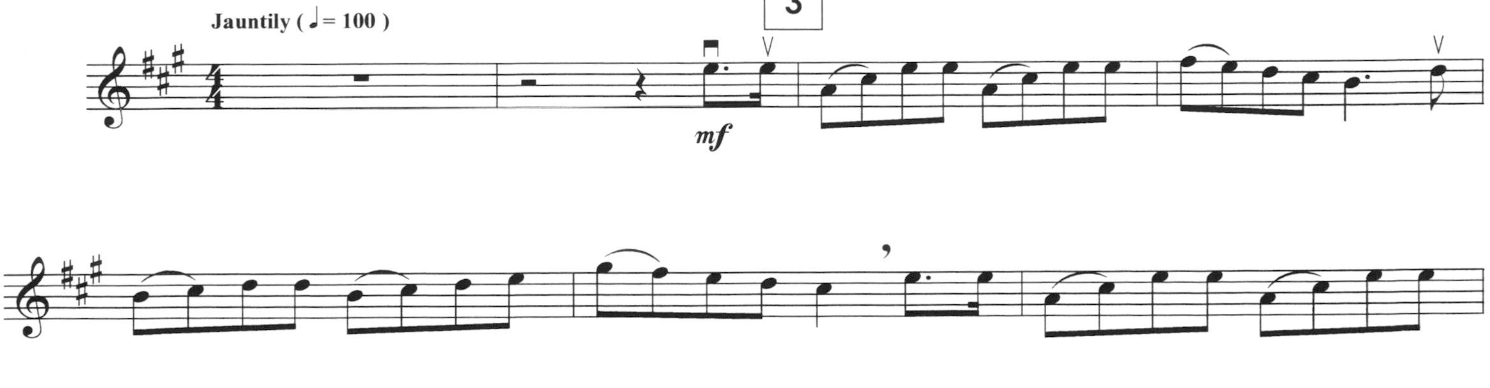

Jauntily (♩ = 100)

4

AIKEN DRUM

Scottish Folk Song
Arr. Timothy Campbell (ASCAP)

TABLE OF CONTENTS

 *Tracks with solo part and accompaniment*

Tracks with accompaniment only

CURNOW MUSIC

JAMES CURNOW
TIMOTHY CAMPBELL

EXCLUSIVELY DISTRIBUTED BY
HAL•LEONARD CORPORATION
7777 W. BLUEMOUND RD., P.O. BOX 13819 MILWAUKEE, WI 53213

FOR ALL AGES

CELTIC FOLKSONGS

Position 1-3

VIOLIN

TIMOTHY CAMPBELL
JAMES CURNOW

CURNOW
MUSIC®

EXCLUSIVELY DISTRIBUTED BY
HAL•LEONARD®
CORPORATION
7777 W. BLUEMOUND RD. P.O. BOX 13819 MILWAUKEE, WI 53213

CELTIC
FOLKSONGS

FOR ALL AGES

PIANO ACCOMPANIMENT

Order Number: CMP 1044-05-400

James Curnow, Timothy Campbell
Celtic Folksongs for all ages
Violin & Piano Accompaniment

CD Accompaniment tracks created by James L. Hosay

CD number: 19-081-3 CMP
ISBN 90-431-2328-5

CELTIC FOLK SONGS FOR ALL AGES

INTRODUCTION

This book is a sampling of rich tunes and ballads specifically distinctive to the cultures of Scotland, Newfoundland and Ireland. Initially associated with everyday rural activities, these memorable melodies have been married with colorful accompaniments to offer a variety of musical settings for all performers.

The accompaniment CD provides all musicians the opportunity to perform for organized gatherings or spontaneous productions among friends and relatives. There are two tracks for each tune. The first track includes a sample performance of the solo with the accompaniment. The second track is just the accompaniment, allowing the soloist to play along. So, delight in the richness of *"CELTIC FOLK SONGS FOR ALL AGES"* and continue the spirit with which folk music has been passed down through cultures near and far.

JAMES CURNOW

James Curnow was born in Port Huron, Michigan and raised in Royal Oak, Michigan. He lives in Nicholasville, Kentucky where he is president, composer, and educational consultant for Curnow Music Press, Inc. of Wilmore, Kentucky, publishers of significant music for concert band and brass band. He also serves as Composer-in-residence (Emeritus) on the faculty of Asbury College in Wilmore, Kentucky, and is editor of all music publications for The Salvation Army in Atlanta, Georgia.

His formal training was received at Wayne State University (Detroit, Michigan) and at Michigan State University (East Lansing, Michigan), where he was a euphonium student of Leonard Falcone, and a conducting student of Dr. Harry Begian. His studies in composition and arranging were with F. Maxwell Wood, James Gibb, Jere Hutchinson, and Irwin Fischer.

James Curnow has taught in all areas of instrumental music, both in the public schools (five years), and on the college and university level (twenty-six years). He is a member of several professional organizations, including the American Bandmasters Association, College Band Directors National Association and Wind Ensembles and the American Society of Composers, Authors and Publishers (ASCAP). In 1980 he received the National Band Association's Citation of Excellence. In 1985, while a tenured Associate Professor at the University of Illinois, Champaign-Urbana, Mr. Curnow was honored as an outstanding faculty member. Among his most recent honors are inclusion in Who's Who in America, Who's Who in the South and Southwest, and Composer of the Year (1997) by the Kentucky Music Teachers Association and the National Music Teachers Association. He has received annual ASCAP standard awards since 1979.

As a conductor, composer and clinician, Curnow has traveled throughout the United States, Canada, Australia, Japan and Europe where his music has received wide acclaim. He has won several awards for band compositions including the ASBDA/Volkwein Composition Award in 1977 (*Symphonic Triptych*) and 1979 (*Collage for Band*), the ABA/Ostwald Award in 1980 (*Mutanza*) and 1984 (Symphonic Variants for Euphonium and Band), the 1985 Sixth International Competition of Original Compositions for Band (*Australian Variants Suite*), and the 1994 Coup de Vents Composition Competition of Le Havre, France (*Lochinvar*).

Curnow has been commissioned to write over two hundred works for concert band, brass band, orchestra, choir and various vocal and instrumental ensembles. His published works now number well over four hundred. His most recent commissions include the Tokyo Symphony Orchestra (*Symphonic Variants for Euphonium and Orchestra*), the United States Army Band (Pershing's Own, Washington, D.C.-Lochinvar, Symphonic Poem for Winds and Percussion), Roger Behrend and the DEG Music Products, Inc. and Willson Band Instrument Companies (*Concerto for Euphonium and Orchestra*), the Olympic Fanfare and Theme for the Olympic Flag (Atlanta Committee for the Olympic Games, 1996), the Kentucky Music Teachers Association/National Music Teachers Association in 1997 (*On Poems of John Keats for String Quartet*) and Michigan State University Bands (John Whitwell, Director of Bands) in honor of David Catron's twenty-six years of service to the university and the university bands (*Ode And Epinicion*).

TIMOTHY CAMPBELL

Timothy Campbell was born in Guelph, Ontario, Canada. He currently lives in Manchester, Connecticut where he teaches K – 12 instrumental and choral music for Cornerstone Christian School. He is also the personnel manager and contractor for the Summer Music Festival orchestra in New London, Connecticut, where he has worked with such artists as Jane Glover, Robert Levin, Larry Rachleff, Norman Krieger, Donald Pippen, and Johnny Mathis.

He received his undergraduate degree from Asbury College in theory and composition. While attending Asbury he studied with James Curnow and garnered such accolades as the Kentucky Music Educators Composition Award and the Penniston Honors Competition awards for piano and composition. Under a full scholarship, he went on to the University of Connecticut where he completed his master's degree in music theory.

TABLE OF CONTENTS

AIKEN DRUM

Scottish Folk Song
Arr. **Timothy Campbell** (ASCAP)

AIKEN DRUM 3

BELIEVE ME, IF ALL THOSE
ENDEARING YOUNG CHARMS

Irish Folk Song
Arr. **Timothy Campbell** (ASCAP)

JACK WAS EVERY INCH A SAILOR

Newfoundland Folk Song
Arr. James Curnow (ASCAP)

12

JACK WAS EVERY INCH A SAILOR 2

JACK WAS EVERY INCH A SAILOR 3

THE ASH GROVE

Welsh Folk Song
Arr. Timothy Campbell (ASCAP)

Copyright © 2005 by **Curnow Music Press, Inc.**

THE ASH GROVE 3

I'LL TELL ME MA

Irish Folk Song
Arr. Timothy Campbell (ASCAP)

I'LL TELL ME MA 3

THE BLUEBELLS OF SCOTLAND

Scottish Folk Song
Arr. James Curnow (ASCAP)

Violin

Piano

Moderately slow, flowing (♩ = 96)

Pedal harmonically throughout

mf *legato* *mp* *f* *mp* *p*

THE BLUEBELLS OF SCOTLAND 2

THE BLUEBELLS OF SCOTLAND 3

I'S THE B'Y

Newfoundland Folk Song
Arr. Timothy Campbell (ASCAP)